An Easy-to-Make
GODEY DOLL

with Instructions and
Ready-to-Use Patterns
for a Complete Wardrobe

G.P. Jones

DOVER PUBLICATIONS, INC.
New York

Published in Canada by General Publishing Com-
pany, Ltd., 30 Lesmill Road, Don Mills, Toronto,
Ontario.
Published in the United Kingdom by Constable and
Company, Ltd., 10 Orange Street, London WC2H
7EG.

*An Easy-to-Make Godey Doll with Instructions
and Ready-to-Use Patterns for a Complete Wardrobe*
is a new work, first published by Dover Publications, Inc., in 1978.

International Standard Book Number: 0-486-23710-9
Library of Congress Catalog Card Number: 78-56762

Manufactured in the United States of America
Dover Publications, Inc.
180 Varick Street
New York, N.Y. 10014

Introduction

The doll and her wardrobe in this book are not only easy to make, but are also an authentic introduction to the fashion world of the 1850's. During this decade, women began to assert their independence, taking part in more and more activities outside the home. Lucy Stone organizeed the first National Women's Rights Convention; Elizabeth Blackwell became the first woman in modern times to practice medicine; Susan B. Anthony began her long career for women's rights, and Amelia Bloomer advocated the adoption of a new mode of dress for women, consisting of a dress with short skirts worn over Turkish trousers which became known as "bloomers." (The "bloomer costume" was discussed more than it was worn, and the fad soon faded.)

The average American woman of the 1850's, however, found most of her inspiration in *Godey's Lady's Book,* a nineteenth-century woman's magazine which was devoted to women's interests and domestic life and which reflected the manners and morals of the day. During the 1850's the circulation of the magazine reached over 150,000. My doll version of an 1850's lady has a face, hairdo and wardrobe taken directly from the pages of *Godey's.* Her clothes have been simplified as much as possible to suit a doll, but she still carries the fashion ideas which were popular at that time.

Godey's often published dressmaking patterns, and the Grecian Cloak on page 24 and the Echarpe Orientale on page 26, are taken from two of these patterns which are reproduced on pages 3 and 4.

The home seamstress was expected to enlarge the tiny drawings to make her own full-size patterns as well as to follow the sometimes impossible directions. Not only that, but it appears that the engraver took considerable license when rendering the illustrations. There is no way that the fullness indicated in the pattern for the Grecian Cloak could be shaped into the perfectly smooth sleeve cap as shown in the illustration. The Grecian Cloak also has a pattern for what appears to be a double collar, but there are no directions given

as to how it is to be attached or closed. I have omitted the collar from the doll version and closed the neck of the cloak with a ribbon.

Just for fun try reading the directions given with the original patterns before you try the doll version. Imagine that you are considering the garment for yourself, and decide if you would be willing to risk eight or nine yards of precious fabric for making up the design. I think you will look at our modern patterns with more reverence the next time you begin a big sewing project.

I have done both patterns in fairly light colors so that the details can be seen in the photographs. However, deep colors such as black, brown or maroon would be more suitable for the cloak. The Echarpe Orientale could be done in light colors for the summer, but a dark shade from the dress it will cover would be more suitable.

All of the pattern pieces for the doll and her wardrobe are printed on special lightweight pattern paper in the special pattern section following page 12. Since these patterns are printed on one side only, they can be cut out and used as you would any commercial dress pattern. The solid line is the cutting line; the dashed line is the sewing line.

To transfer the necessary markings on the pattern to the fabric, use dressmaker's carbon or graphite paper. Do not use typewriter carbon; it will smudge and rub off on the fabric and is almost impossible to remove. Dressmaker's carbon, available at notion, fabric and dime stores, comes in packs of assorted colors in strips about 7" x 20". It has a hard, waxy finish and is designed for this purpose. Trace the hands and the other sewing instructions such as notches, dots and darts on the *wrong* side of the fabric. Trace the features and hairline on the *right* side of the fabric. Try to trace lightly, applying just enough pressure so that you can see the lines without their showing through the fabric.

For the doll bodies, choose a tightly woven fabric, such as broadcloth or poplin. Percale is often suggested; however, I find that it is too thin to be stuffed as tightly as a doll should be stuffed to hold its shape. The better the grade of fabric used, the more satisfied you will be with the results. I prefer to use a pale peach color rather than a pink. It looks more natural.

For clothing, look for fabrics that are drapeable, but at the same time will not ravel easily. Keep in mind that the pattern pieces are small and will ravel with handling. For example, a poor choice would be crepe-back satin, as it will ravel before you can get it sewn. You can, however, use regular satin. Cotton lining will do nicely as a substitute for hard-to-find colored batiste.

When choosing prints or plaids, keep them small, in scale with the doll's size. For trims, try to use laces that have the look of hand crochet or tatting.

If you enjoy handstitching, embroidery, crocheting, tatting, and so forth, you can make the wardrobe more elaborate and even more authentic, by indulging in these arts for trims and decoration of the costumes. Keep in mind that these are basic patterns and can be made just as elaborate as your own imagination will allow.

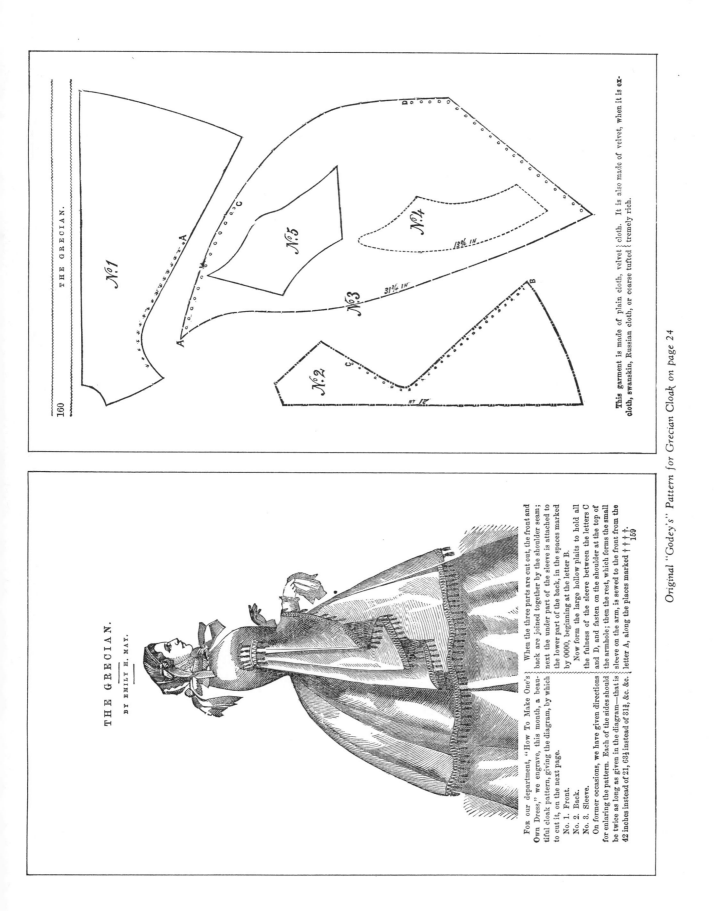

THE GRECIAN.
160

N.º 1

A——A

C

N.º 5

N.º 4
13¾ IN.

N.º 3
31¾ IN.

D

B

N.º 2
C
HT 12

This garment is made of plain cloth, velvet } cloth. It is also made of velvet, when it is ex-
cloth, swanskin, Russian cloth, or coarse tufted } tremely rich.

THE GRECIAN.
BY EMILY H. MAY.

For our department, "How To Make One's Own Dress," we engrave, this month, a beautiful cloak pattern, giving the diagram, by which to cut it, on the next page.

No. 1. Front.
No. 2. Back.
No. 3. Sleeve.

On former occasions, we have given directions for enlarging the pattern. Each of the sides should be twice as long as given in the diagram—that is 42 inches instead of 21, 68½ instead of 31¼, &c. &c.

When the three parts are cut out, the front and back are joined together by the shoulder seam; next the under part of the sleeve is attached to the lower part of the back, in the spaces marked by 0000, beginning at the letter B.

Now form the large hollow plaits to hold all the fulness of the sleeve between the letters C and D, and fasten on the shoulder at the top of the armhole; then the rest, which forms the small sleeve on the arm, is sewed to the front from the letter A, along the places marked † † †.
169

Original "Godey's" Pattern for Grecian Cloak on page 24

to the dress just above figure No. 1, in front of the shoulder; a couple of moderately wide ribbon strings fasten it at the waist, more or less shut according to the form of the wearer; and a brooch to keep this knot steadily fixed is advisable. Much depends on wearing a dress properly, without which precaution the best shaped article will fall the wrong way.

The *Echarpe Orientale* seems likely to remain long a favorite in the gay city of Paris, and to supersede all others, for the simple reason that, without being remarkable, or *outre* in appearance, it shows off the figure to the best possible advantage. Any young lady can understand, by referring to an inch measure, how to cut it. The artist having numbered the *inches* exactly, all that is requisite is to have a long tape with inches marked on it, to refer to when cutting out.

To make an *Echarpe Orientale* according to the pattern given, (being that suited to a lady of ordinary size) four yards of black glace silk, three quarters of a yard wide, is necessary; but should the height of the person, and width of the bust and shoulders be greater, more will be required, as the first frill and trimming must begin from the waist, and that in front must end within a quarter of a yard of the knee.

Having cut the pattern in paper, or old linen, according to the measurement given, it will be well to try it on the figure, and remark whether any alteration is necessary. The principal matter to be observed is, that the slight gatherings indicated on the body of the *echarpe*, just above the figure No. 1, should be gathered gradually to fit nicely round the front part of the shoulder, becoming plain again at the curved part, which is rounded so as to rest on the bust.

This done, the frills should have hems folded back of about one inch in width, and black velvet ribbon of the same breadth placed above them. No. 2 should then be quilled in flat plaits of two inches wide, having one inch of space between each plait, and fastened down on the line marked C E, the letters on the frill being placed exactly on those corresponding on the *echarpe*. No. 4 must be plaited, and placed in exactly the same manner, only it must pass beyond No. 2 (at the turn of the arm) so as to let the hem and trimming be seen beyond. No. 3 crosses *under*, reaching to E, which finishes the mantle nicely, and allows a free passage for the arm at the part alluded to. This frill has three plaits the same width as the others at the bottom of the mantle, and one at the corner; but the rest, as far as the letter F, is plain. This done, a similar band of ribbon velvet should be placed all round at the edge of the *echarpe*, so as to finish it neatly, that above the frills resting upon the first.

As the black glace silk used for those *echarpes* ought to be good, no lining is required; but as our climate is much more variable than that of France, it is well to provide against it. Thus, in winter, a lining can be added; only be sure it is cut out and tacked on so as to fit the *echarpe* exactly, and, as the chest is uncovered, a thick, high jacket (or *basquine*) should be worn with it, or at least a piece of wadding or flannel over the chest.

For summer spotted white muslin made up in this way is very light and pretty, and can be made to look more dressy if wanted for a *fête* or promenade, by having plain rose-colored, blue, light green, or lilac ribbon inserted the hems, where they are indicated in the figure given. Others may be made of plain muslin, with hems of the same. Others of the same material with worked frills, or with light embroidered sprigs on the scarf, and frills of a pattern to match.

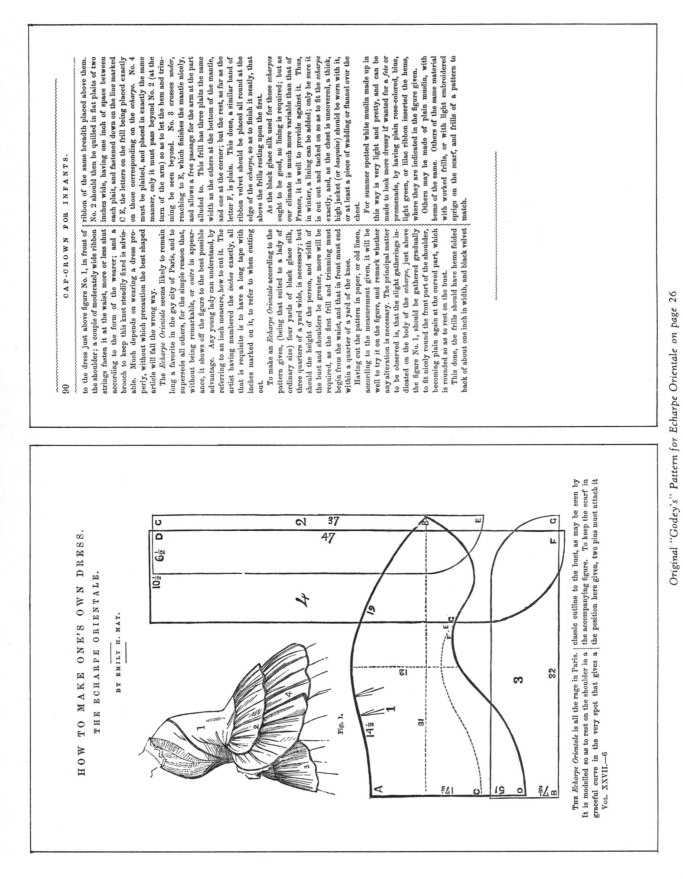

HOW TO MAKE ONE'S OWN DRESS.
THE ECHARPE ORIENTALE.
BY EMILY H. MAY.

Fig. 1.

THE *Echarpe Orientale* is all the rage in Paris. It is modelled so as to rest on the shoulder in a graceful curve in the very spot that gives a classic outline to the bust, as may be seen by the accompanying figure. To keep the scarf in the position here given, two pins must attach it

Original "Godey's" Pattern for Echarpe Orientale on page 26

DOLL BODY

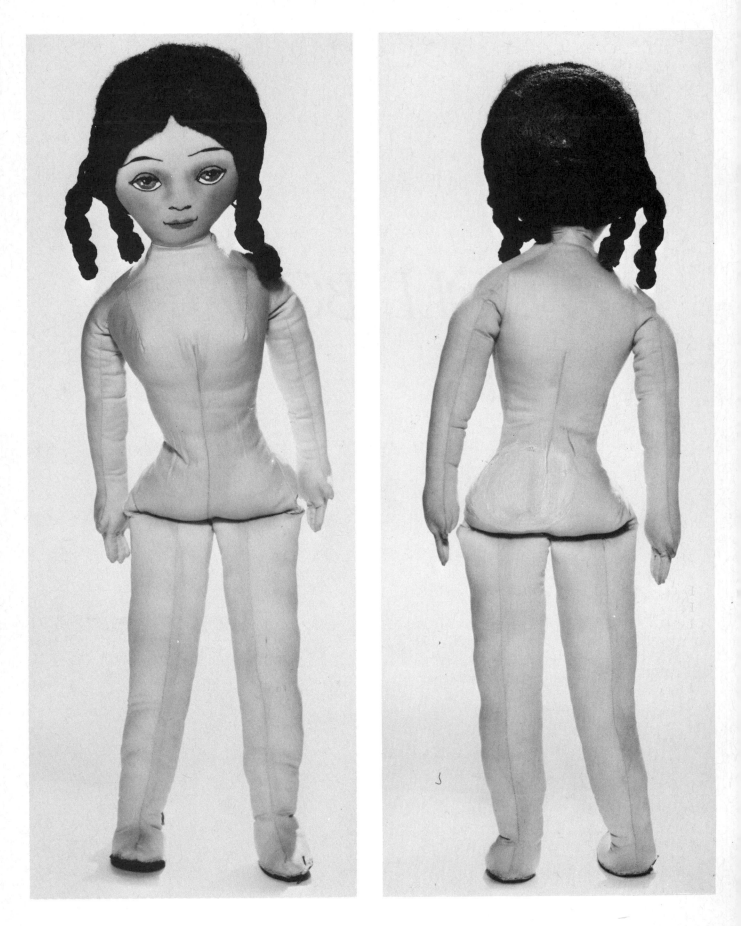

The pattern pieces for the doll are on Plates 1, 2, 3, 4, 5, 6 and 7.

Doll Body

Your doll has a beautifully molded "lady" body. It is easy to construct, but you must cut and sew accurately to achieve the desired results. Stuffing is the most important part of making a fashion doll. The doll must be stuffed as tightly as possible, so that she will hold her shape and wear her clothes well.

After you have stuffed the doll, you are ready to embroider the features and apply the hair, according to the instructions given below. After making countless dolls, I have found that the best results are obtained by embroidering the features *after* stuffing. Embroidering the features first often results in a puckered face.

If you use a knot in your embroidery or leave even a tiny tail, it will show through the fabric. When the embroidery is done on a properly stuffed head after the doll is finished, the tension of the stitches is exactly right and no tails or knots can show through. Hair must be done after stuffing because seams are covered with stitches. This technique of embroidering the hair on makes the styles permanent so that when the doll is played with, the hair style is not disturbed. All stitching should be done just under the "skin" so that there is little or no problem with catching in the stuffing.

MATERIALS

2/3 yard flesh-colored fabric
Matching thread
2 ounces sport-weight yarn *(for hair)*
Embroidery thread: medium blue, pink, medium brown
Permanent fine-line markers: black, blue
Dry (powdered) makeup: pink, grey, brown, white
   (for shading face)
Acrylic paints: black, white
Very fine brush
Popsicle stick *(for neck)*
Scraps of plastic *(for soles of feet)*
   NOTE: Face can also be painted. Substitute paint colors for embroidery thread colors.

DIRECTIONS

1. Sew darts in body front and back. Clip center of curved darts.

2. Sew body front to body back at side seams.

3. Sew underarm pieces to body side seams, matching dot on underarm to body side seam. (Underarm pieces should be inside body while sewing, right sides facing.) Clip entire seam where just stitched, being careful not to clip thread.

4. Before cutting head-upper arm pieces, join the pattern pieces where indicated on the pattern. Sew head-upper arm pieces from dot to dot where indicated on pattern.

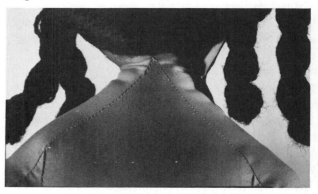

Back of Doll's Neck

5. Beginning at center back neck, baste head-upper arm to body and underarm. Sew, stitching carefully around hands. End stitching at dot at the front side of the neck; do *not* stitch to the raw edge of the fabric.

7

Clip carefully along neck edges, front and back, and between fingers. Carefully trim fingers close to stitching.

6. Machine baste between stars on the lower part of the face. Pull up gathers just enough to ease, but not to form pleats. Concentrate these gathers as much as possible at the chin area. Stitch to the head, matching dots at the top and the chin. Pay particular attention to the seam at the front neck. It must be clipped, so that it will not form a pucker when turned.

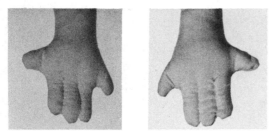

Doll's Hands

7. Turn right-side out.

8. Stitch legs at front and back. Leave foot open to stuff. Turn.

9. Sew legs to lower body back, being sure that toes will face front after stitching.

10. Sew lower body front closed across tops of legs.

11. Begin stuffing through the opening in the head. *You must stuff firmly.* Stuff the fingers and arms first. The arms can be jointed at the elbows by stitching across before the top of the arm is stuffed. Then stuff the body, neck and head. If your doll will be played with, you may want to insert a reinforcement in the neck. A popsicle stick is a good choice; do not use sharp pointed objects or wire. Stuff as tightly as you can. A blunt tool of some sort is a help; I use a long artist's brush with a small rounded tip that will not pierce the fabric.

12. Sew head opening closed.

13. Stuff legs through feet. If you wish your doll to bend at the knees, stuff to just above the knee; stitch across; complete stuffing of the leg down to the foot.

14. Run a hand-gathering stitch around the sole of the foot. Insert the plastic sole and pull up the gathers. Slip stitch the sole to the foot, adding more stuffing for a good, firm foot. Paint on shoes or boots.

15. Paint the whites of the eyes with white acrylic. Let dry.

16. Embroider the irises with medium blue, using two strands of embroidery floss and satin stitch.

17. Fill in pupils with black marker. With blue pen lightly stroke the edges of the irises to give depth.

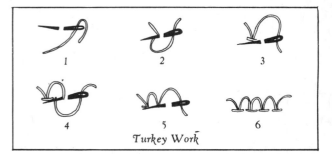

Turkey Work

18. Highlight the irises and pupils with tiny dots of white paint, or, if you prefer, embroider with white.

19. Outline eyes, lids, eyebrows and nose with a single strand of medium brown. The eyelashes are done with a single strand of brown Turkey Work. Put anchoring stitches of Turkey Work next to the eyelids, so that the lashes will point upward.

20. Use two strands of pink, and satin stitch for mouth; then outline mouth opening and laugh lines with a single strand of brown. You can give the face dimension by shading the inner eye and the sides of the nose lightly and rouging cheeks with dry makeup.

21. For hair, work close rows of yarn in back stitch over the entire head. Follow the hairline as indicated on pattern.

Doll's Face

22. Twist a hank of yarn into a "bun" shape and tack securely to the back of the head. For long curls, make two twisted cords with ten strands about 36″ long. Wind matching yarn around and around the center to secure the twists. Tack securely to the top of the head and a portion of the way down the sides to hold in place.

UNDERWEAR

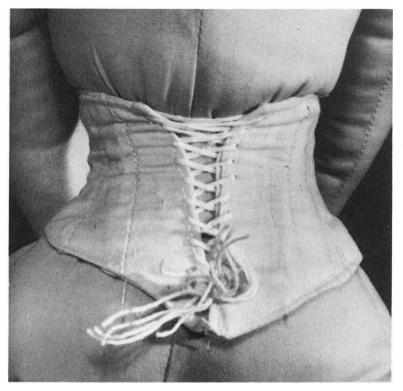

The pattern pieces for the corset are on Plate 8.

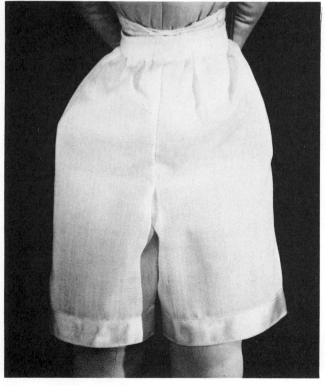

The pattern piece for the pantalettes is on Plate 9.

Petticoat or Crinoline

Underwear

CORSET

A corset cover was often worn over the corset. If you wish to make one, use the front and the back pattern pieces for the ball-gown bodice. Make the corset cover of muslin or satin, lined with the same fabric. Lace the back with a shoelace. The neck and the lower edge can be trimmed with narrow lace ruffling, if you wish.

MATERIALS

¼ yard heavy-weight satin or twill
½ yard feather boning (for bones)
Matching thread
String or cording (for laces)

DIRECTIONS

NOTE: *The corset and the lining are made in the same way.*

1. Fold darts along solid lines; stitch darts in fronts and backs along dashed lines.

2. Sew the boning to the lining pieces along the darts.

3. Sew side seams.

4. Press up seam allowance along the lower edge of the lining and the corset.

5. Right sides together, sew the corset and the lining together, leaving open at the lower (pressed) edge. Turn right-side out.

6. Topstitch all around the corset, close to the edge.

7. To lace the corset, begin at the top edges, and using two needles insert thread in each front. Pull up ends even, as though you were lacing a shoe. Lace to the lower edge and tie in a bow.

PANTALETTES

At this point in fashion history, women's pantalettes were completely plain. You can, if you wish, add a flat ribbon to the hem. To do this, press the seam allowance to the right side of the fabric and stitch a narrow ribbon over the raw edge. If you wish a plain edge, press the seam allowance to the wrong side and make a narrow hem along the edge. Then proceed as below.

MATERIALS

¼ yard white batiste or lightweight muslin
White thread
1 yard ⅜" ribbon (optional)
Hook and eye

DIRECTIONS

1. Before cutting pattern, add ¼" seam allowance for hem, as indicated on the pattern.

2. Sew leg seams on each piece. (see diagram)

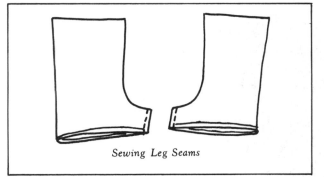

Sewing Leg Seams

3. Turn one piece right-side out and insert inside the other piece, matching leg seams.

4. Stitch both center backs to center fronts in one continuous seam, leaving back open above dots.

5. Turn right-side out.

6. Measure doll's waist (with corset on) and cut a waistband 1½" by waist measure, plus 1".

7. Run a row of gathering stitches along the top seam line and gather the waist of the pantalettes, turning in the seam allowance at the back opening. Pull up gathers to fit the waistband, less 1½".

8. Allowing a ¼" overhang at the beginning of the waistband (for seam), sew the waistband to the

pantalettes, right sides facing. Press all thicknesses towards the waistband.

9. Turn in and press a ¼" seam allowance on the long side of the waistband. Fold waistband in half lengthwise, right sides together, and sew ends. Trim and turn.

10. Slip stitch remaining long end of waistband to inside. Close with hook and eye.

PETTICOAT OR CRINOLINE

Dresses of this period were worn over a type of hoop skirt called a crinoline which was originally made of horsehair and linen thread. The doll version of this undergarment, made of illusion or net, will give the same effect and serve to expand the skirts worn over it.

MATERIALS

1 yard 72" wide illusion or net
White thread
3" x 10" scrap of white batiste or muslin
Hook and eye

DIRECTIONS

1. Cut the following tiers from the 36" end of the illusion or net:

1 tier 7" x 36"	1 tier 21" x 36"
1 tier 13" x 36"	2 tiers 7" x 36"

2. Sew two of the 7" x 36" tiers together along one short side. Fold in half lengthwise and baste raw edges together on the long side and on one short side. Gather the long, raw edge to measure 36". Set aside to use as a ruffle on the bottom.

3. Fold the remaining tiers in half lengthwise and baste along the long, raw edges.

4. With the shortest tier on top, align all the long, raw edges and run three rows of machine basting through all thicknesses of the three tiers. One row should be right on the seam line, one inside the seam allowance, and one outside the seam line. This will hold the gathers out of the way while applying the waistband.

5. Measure doll's waist (with corset on) and cut a waistband 1½" by waist measure, plus 1".

6. Gather the waist of the petticoat, turning in seam allowance at the back opening. Pull up gathers to fit the waistband, less 1½".

7. Allowing a ¼" overhang at the beginning of the waistband (for seam), sew the waistband to the petticoat, right sides facing. Press all thicknesses towards the waistband.

8. Turn in and press a ¼" seam allowance on the long side of waistband. Fold waistband in half lengthwise, right sides together, and sew ends. Trim and turn.

9. Slip stitch remaining long end of waistband to inside.

10. Stuff each tier with strips of illusion or net; then baste the ends closed.

11. Pin the petticoat on the doll. Stuff the remaining tier you set aside to use as a ruffle as you did the others and baste the remaining short end closed. Pin to the lower edge of the petticoat, having the bottom of the last tier about 1" above the floor. Sew in place on the wrong side of the petticoat.

12. Sew up the back seam to within 2" of waistband. Close with hook and eye. Remove gathering stitches which show below the waistband.

INSTRUCTIONS CONTINUE AFTER PATTERNS.

READY-TO-USE PATTERNS

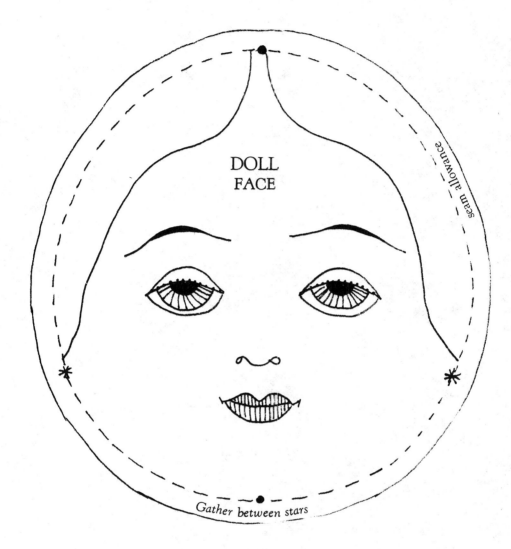

DOLL
FACE

seam allowance

Gather between stars

PLATE 1

PLATE 1

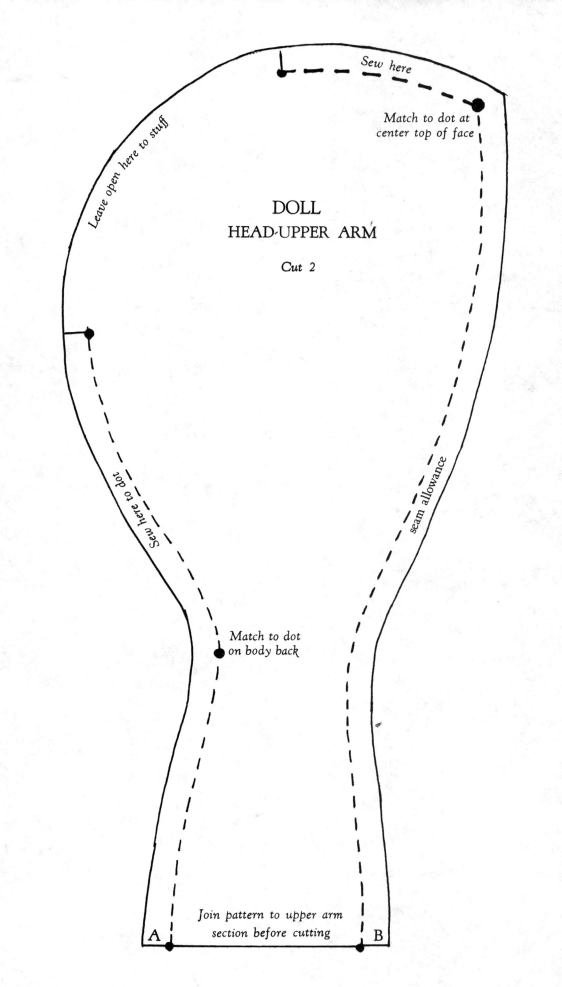

Sew here

Match to dot at
center top of face

Leave open here to stuff

DOLL
HEAD-UPPER ARM

Cut 2

Sew here to dot

seam allowance

Match to dot
on body back

Join pattern to upper arm
section before cutting

A   B

PLATE 2

A B

Join pattern to head
section before cutting

DOLL
HEAD·UPPER ARM

Cut 2

seam allowance

PLATE 3

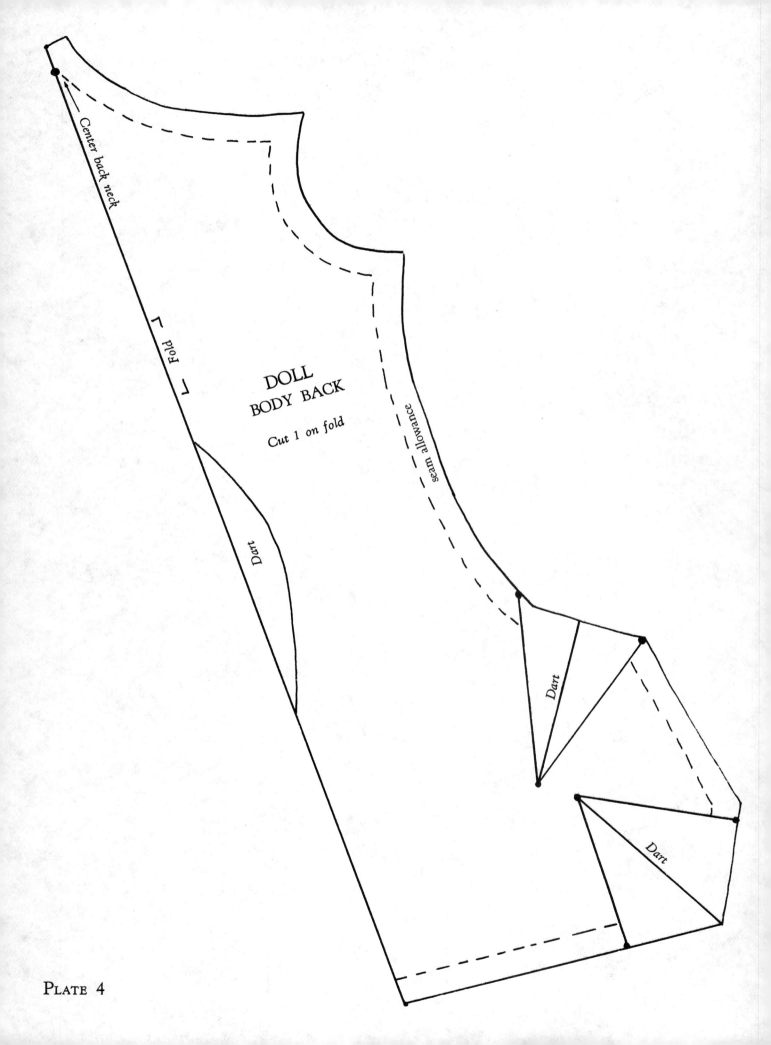

DOLL
BODY BACK

Cut 1 on fold

Center back neck

Fold

Dart

seam allowance

Dart

Dart

PLATE 4

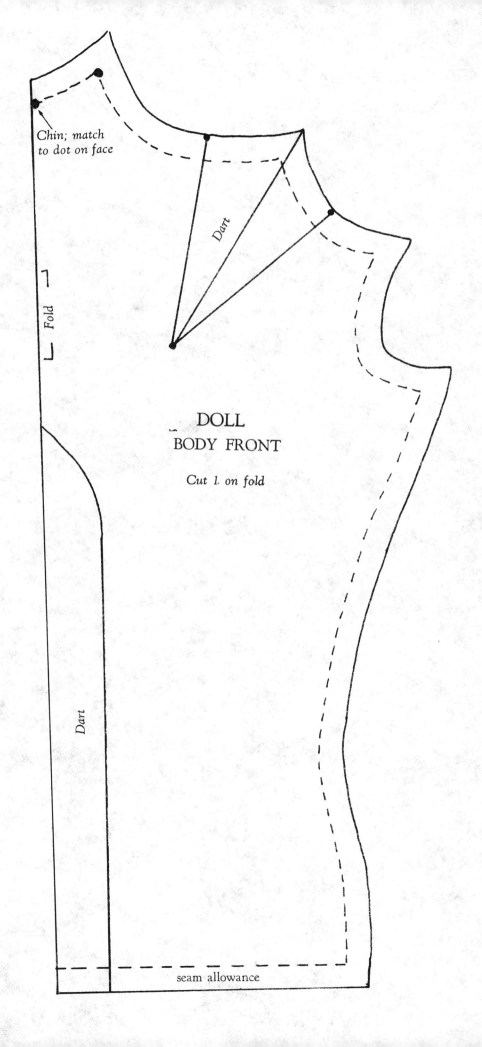

Chin; match
to dot on face

Fold

Dart

DOLL
BODY FRONT

Cut 1 on fold

Dart

seam allowance

PLATE 5

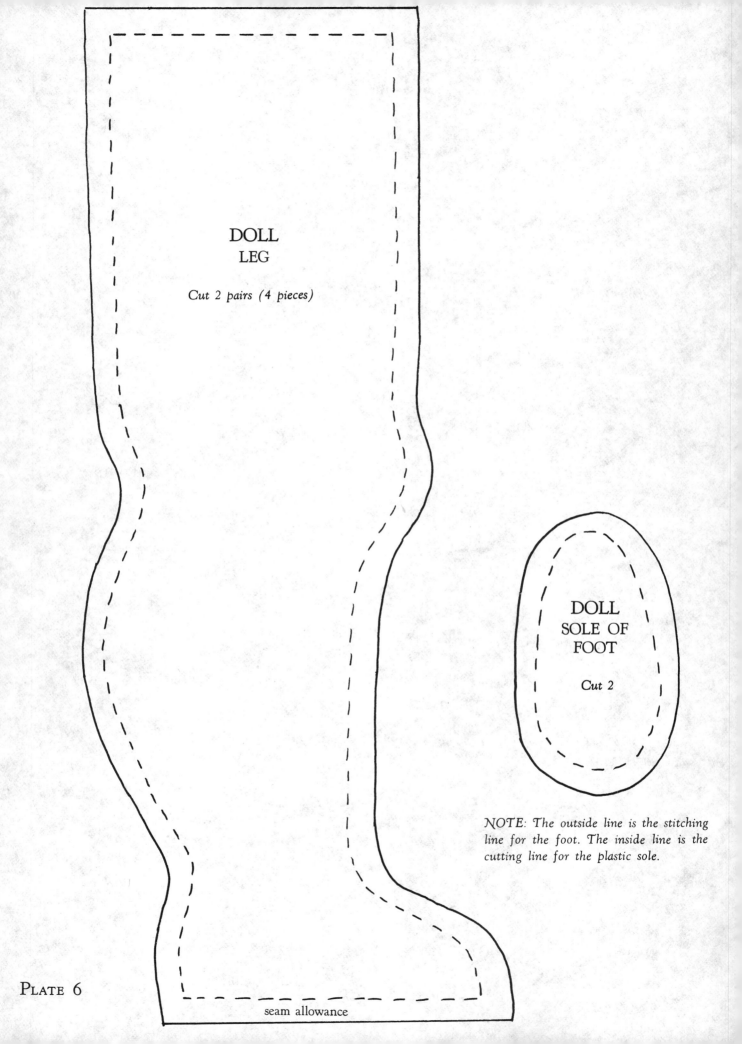

DOLL
LEG

Cut 2 pairs (4 pieces)

DOLL
SOLE OF
FOOT

Cut 2

NOTE: The outside line is the stitching line for the foot. The inside line is the cutting line for the plastic sole.

PLATE 6

seam allowance

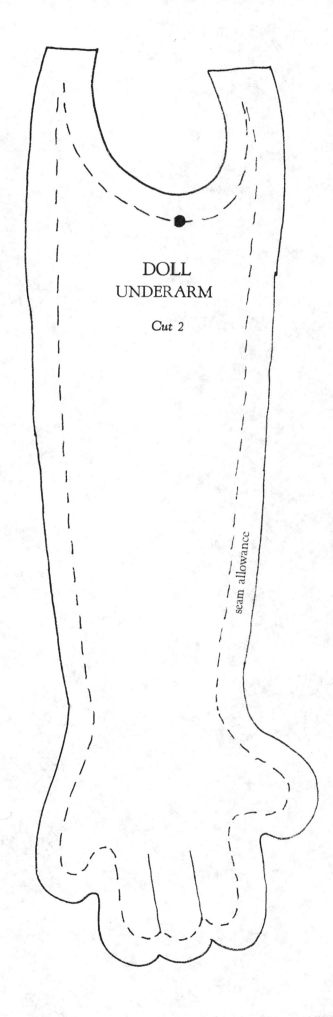

DOLL
UNDERARM

Cut 2

seam allowance

PLATE 7

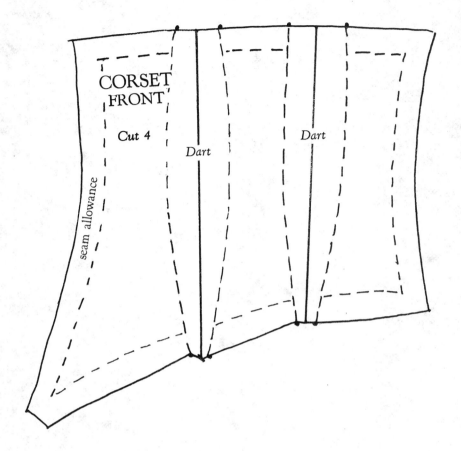

CORSET
FRONT

Cut 4

Dart

Dart

seam allowance

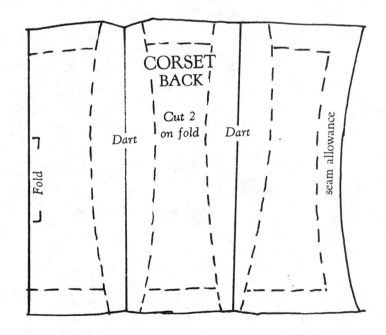

CORSET
BACK

Cut 2
on fold

Dart

Dart

Fold

seam allowance

PLATE 8

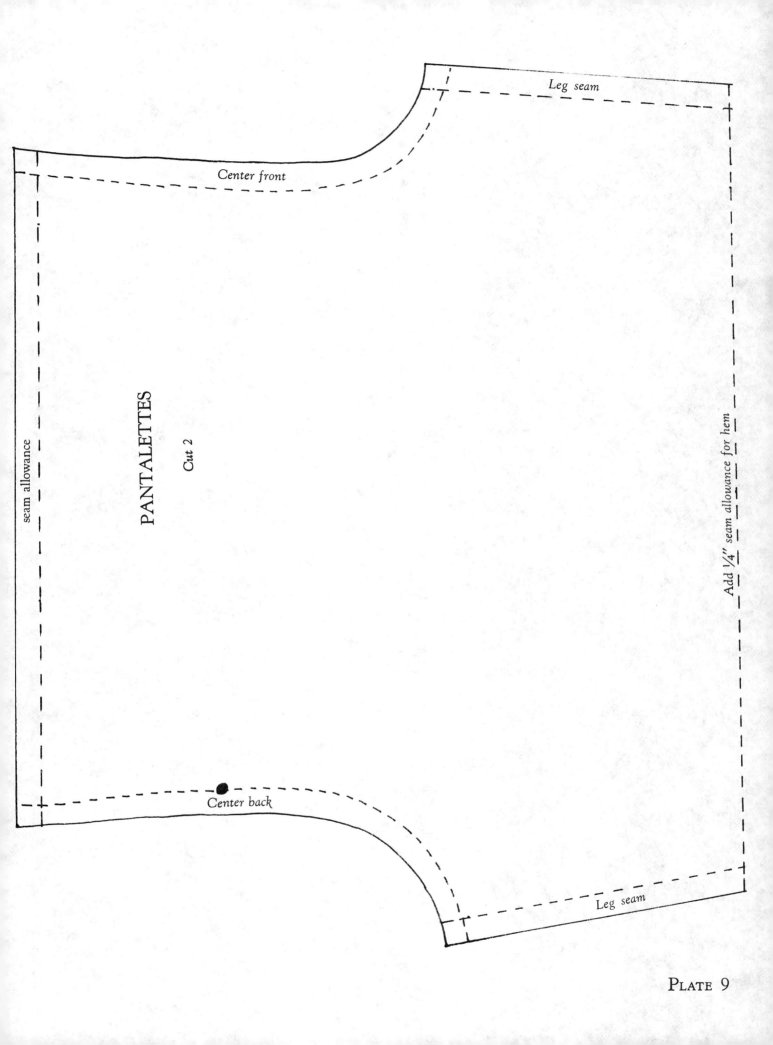

Leg seam

Center front

seam allowance

PANTALETTES

Cut 2

Add ¼″ seam allowance for hem

Center back

Leg seam

PLATE 9

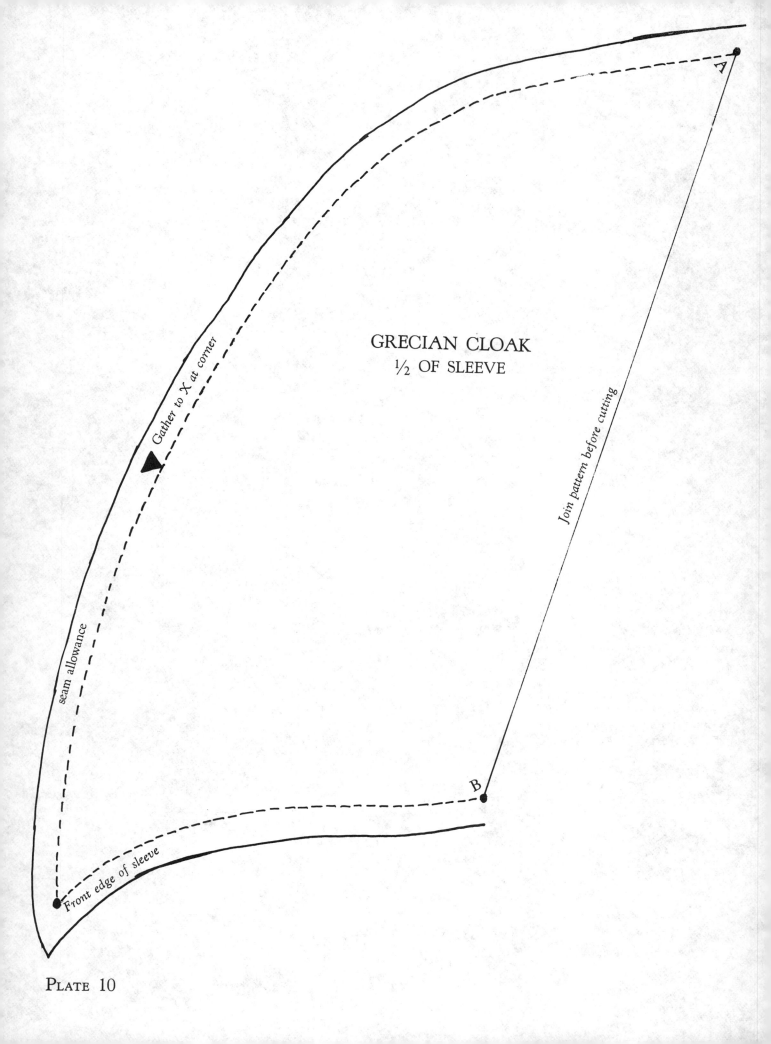

GRECIAN CLOAK
½ OF SLEEVE

Gather to X at corner

seam allowance

Join pattern before cutting

A

B

Front edge of sleeve

PLATE 10

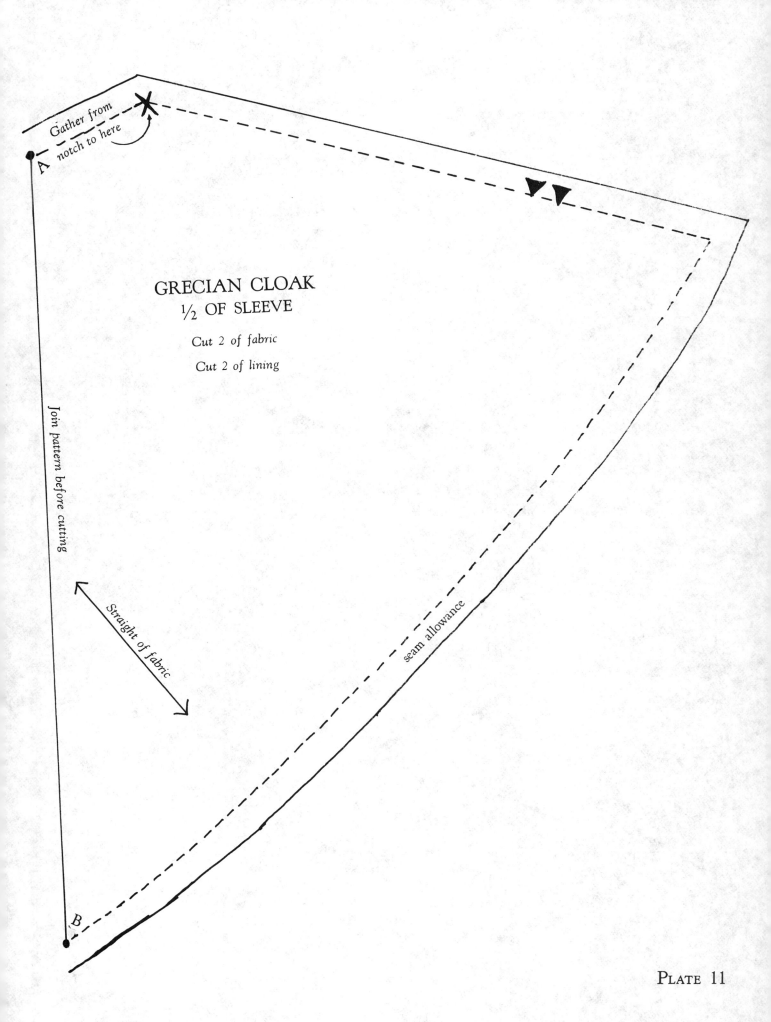

Gather from
notch to here

A

Join pattern before cutting

GRECIAN CLOAK
½ OF SLEEVE

Cut 2 of fabric

Cut 2 of lining

Straight of fabric

seam allowance

B

PLATE 11

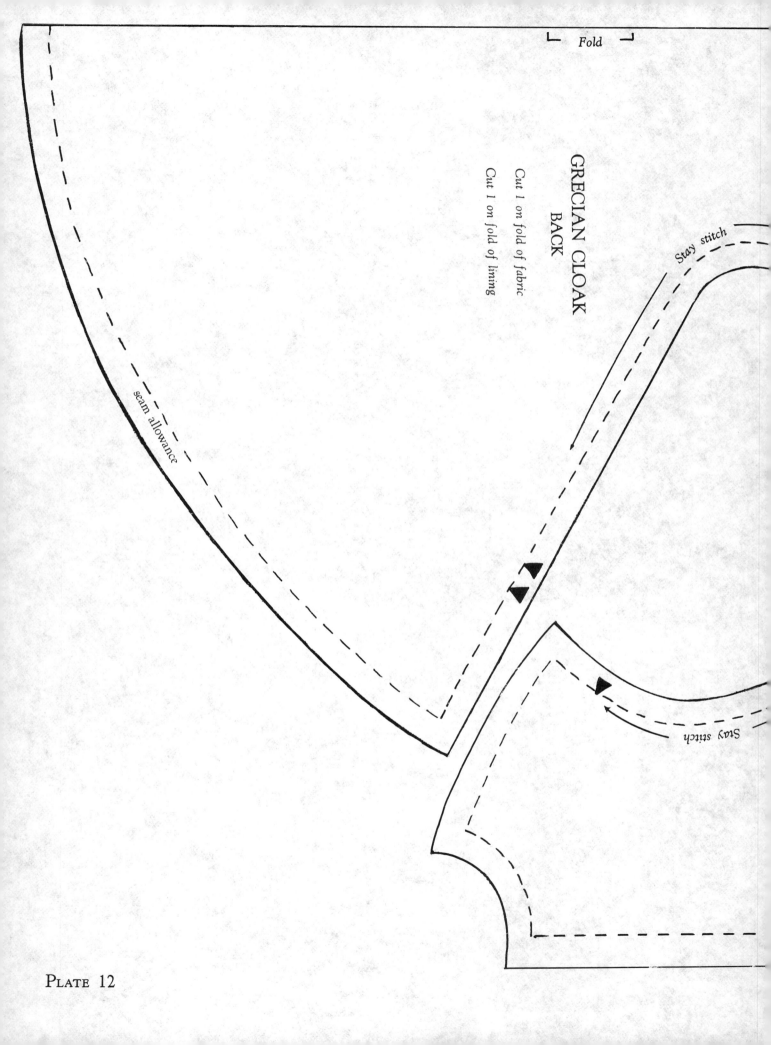

Fold

GRECIAN CLOAK
BACK

Cut 1 on fold of fabric

Cut 1 on fold of lining

Stay stitch

seam allowance

Stay stitch

PLATE 12

GRECIAN CLOAK
FRONT

Cut 2 of fabric

Cut 2 of lining

seam allowance

PLATE 13

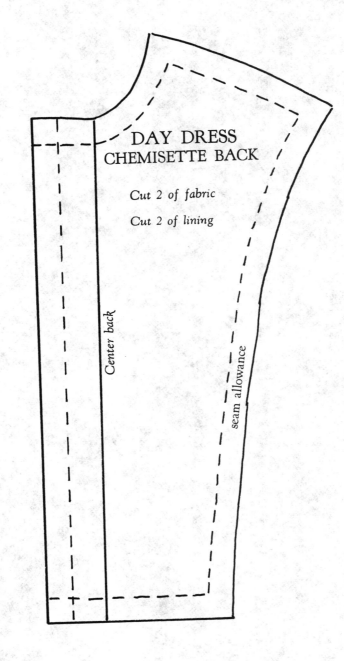

DAY DRESS
CHEMISETTE BACK

Cut 2 of fabric

Cut 2 of lining

Center back

seam allowance

PLATE 14

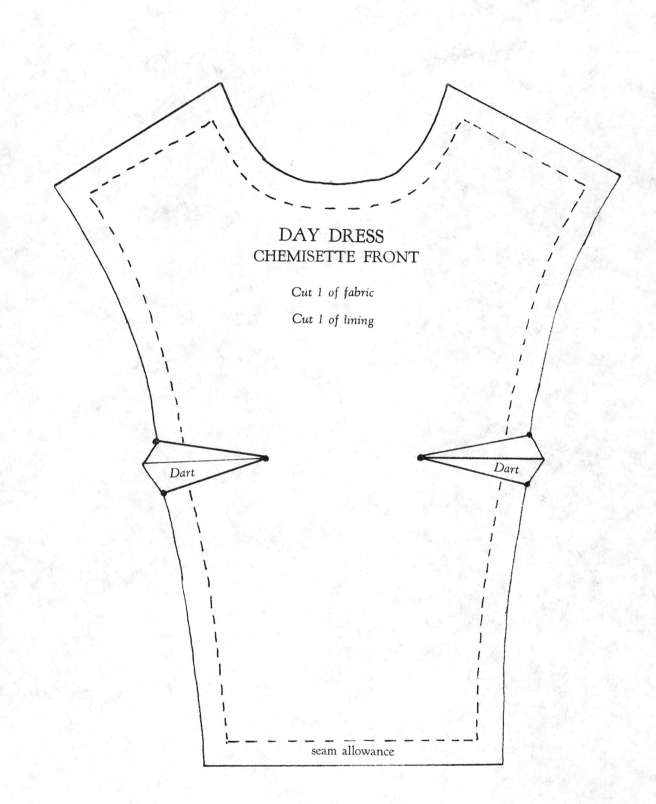

DAY DRESS
CHEMISETTE FRONT

Cut 1 of fabric

Cut 1 of lining

Dart

Dart

seam allowance

PLATE 15

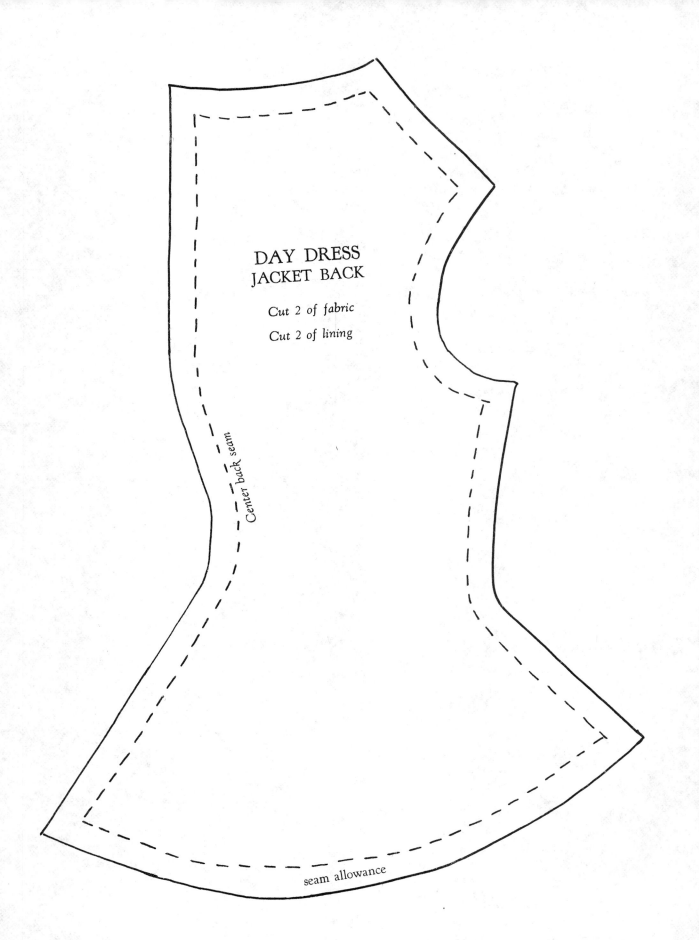

DAY DRESS
JACKET BACK

Cut 2 of fabric

Cut 2 of lining

Center back seam

seam allowance

PLATE 16

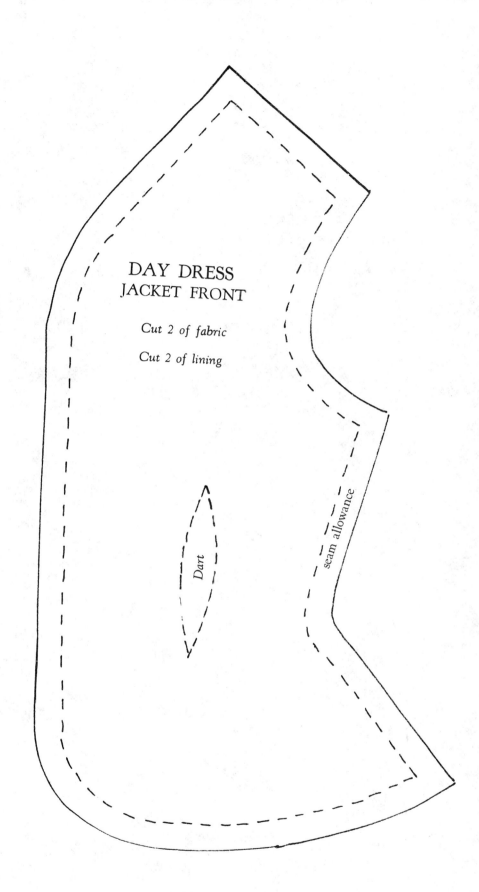

DAY DRESS
JACKET FRONT

Cut 2 of fabric

Cut 2 of lining

Dart

seam allowance

PLATE 17

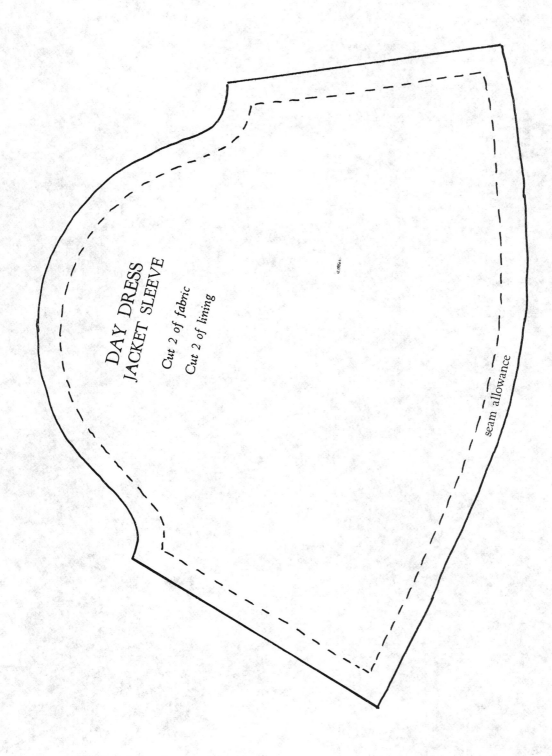

DAY DRESS
JACKET SLEEVE

Cut 2 of fabric

Cut 2 of lining

seam allowance

PLATE 18

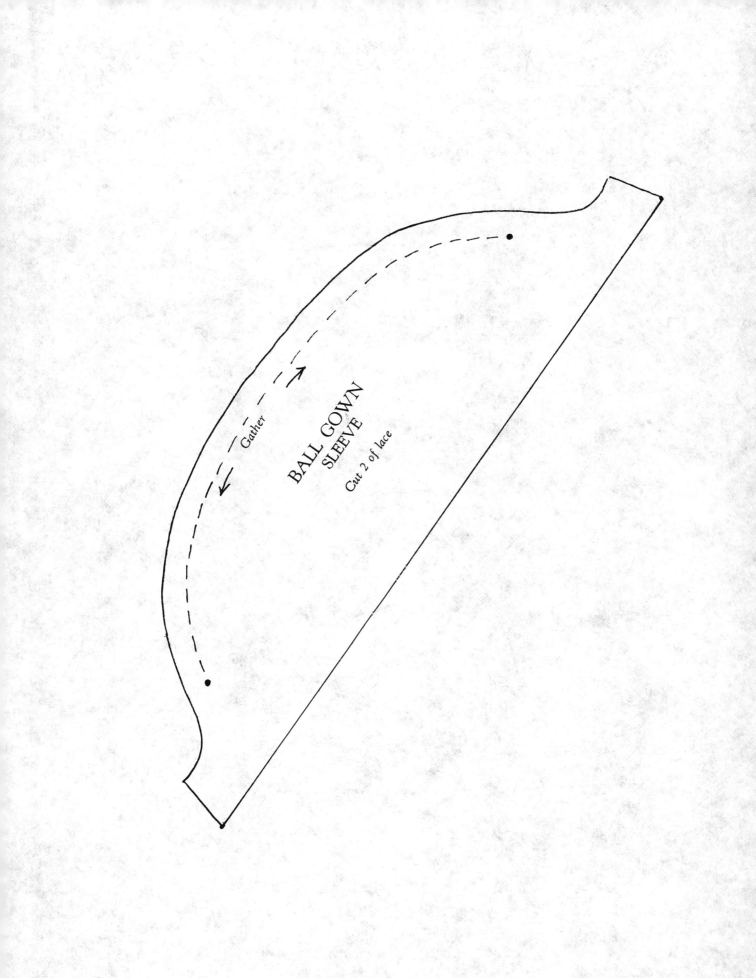

BALL GOWN
SLEEVE

Cut 2 of lace

Gather

PLATE 19

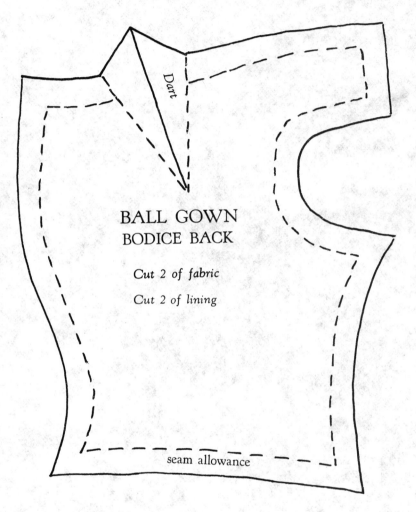

BALL GOWN
BODICE BACK

Cut 2 of fabric

Cut 2 of lining

Dart

seam allowance

PLATE 20

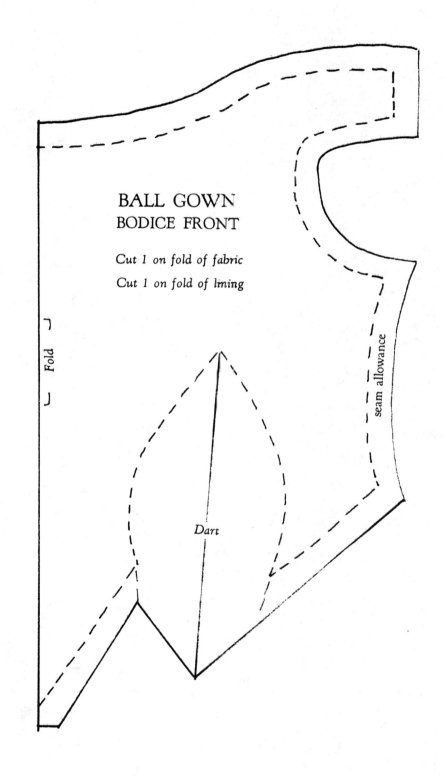

BALL GOWN
BODICE FRONT

Cut 1 on fold of fabric

Cut 1 on fold of lining

Fold

seam allowance

Dart

PLATE 21

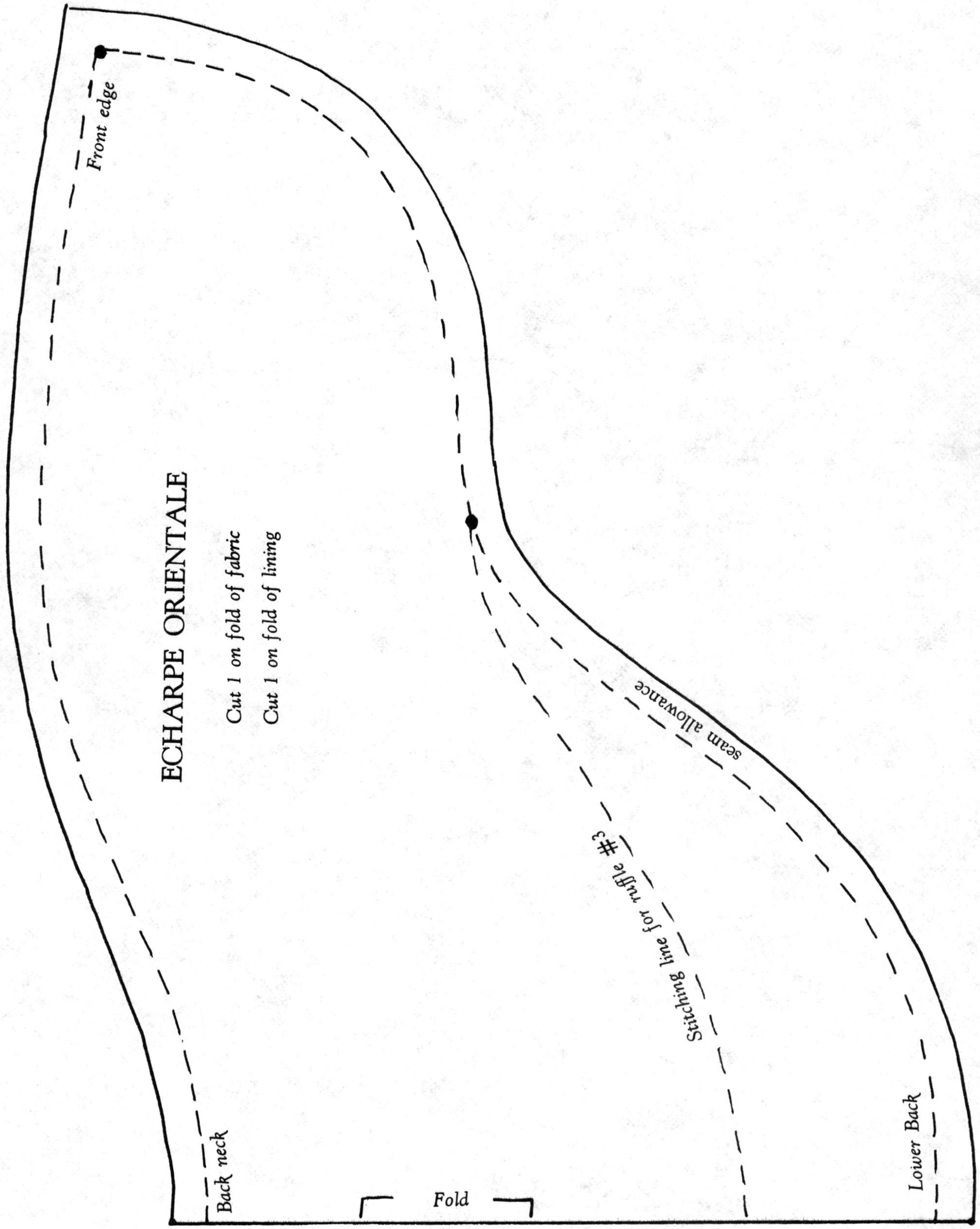

ECHARPE ORIENTALE

Cut 1 on fold of fabric

Cut 1 on fold of lining

Front edge

Back neck

seam allowance

Stitching line for ruffle #3

Lower Back

Fold

PLATE 22

Folded edge

ECHARPE ORIENTALE
CUTTING GUIDE FOR END OF RUFFLE #4

Cut 1 29" x 6"

Raw edge

PLATE 23

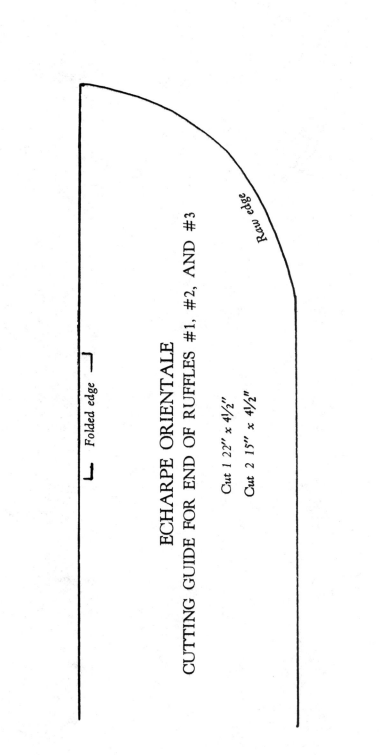

ECHARPE ORIENTALE

CUTTING GUIDE FOR END OF RUFFLES #1, #2, AND #3

Cut 1 22" x 4½"

Cut 2 15" x 4½"

Folded edge

Raw edge

PLATE 24

WARDROBE

The pattern pieces for the dress are on Plates 14, 15,16, 17 and 18.

Blue Brocade Day Dress

The day dress is adapted from one of the charming hand-colored fashion engravings, reproduced on page 16, which appeared each month in *Godey's*. The outfit consisted of a wide skirt and jacket worn over a chemisette which was the forerunner of our modern dickey. Costumes of this period had separate sleeves which were fastened above the elbow and worn under the jacket. This would be too bulky for a doll so the sleeves are attached here to the jacket lining as a trim.

MATERIALS

1 yard blue brocade *(at least 40" wide)*
Matching thread
Hook and eye *(for skirt)*
1/4 yard lining *(for jacket)*
2 yards black looped braid trim *(for jacket)*
2 yards 3" white cotton lace *(for jacket)*
2 yards narrow black velvet ribbon
1/4 yard white batiste or muslin *(for chemisette)*
2 yards 1/4" white lace ruffling *(for chemisette)*
5 inches 3/4" elastic *(for chemisette)*
Snaps
Post earring for pierced ears *(optional)*

DIRECTIONS

Skirt

1. Cut the skirt 18" by the width of the fabric.
2. Run a row of gathering stitches along one long side.
3. Measure doll's waist (with corset on) and cut a waistband 1 1/2" by waist measure plus 1".
4. Gather the skirt, turning in the seam allowance at the back opening. Pull up gathers to fit the waistband, less 1 1/2".
5. Allowing a 1/4" overhang at the beginning of the waistband, sew the waistband to the skirt, right sides facing. Press all thicknesses toward the waistband.
6. Turn in and press a 1/4" seam allowance on the long side of the waistband. Fold the waistband in half, lengthwise, right sides together and sew ends. Trim and turn.

7. Slip stitch remaining long end of the waistband to the inside.
8. Sew up back seam and hem skirt. Hem should be just barely above the floor. Close with hook and eye.

Jacket

1. Cut one jacket of brocade and one of lining.
2. Sew darts in jacket fronts.
3. Sew center back seam. Clip at waist.
4. Join jacket fronts to jacket back at shoulders.
5. Press all seams open.
6. Sew braid to the lower edge of the sleeve with raw edges even. Press seam allowance at the lower edge of the sleeve to the inside.
7. Set in sleeve, sewing with the sleeve on the bottom, next to the machine.
8. Sew underarm sleeve seam and side seam in one continuous seam. Clip at waist.
9. Press seams open, except for sleeve cap which is not pressed.
10. Sew braid to the entire outside edge with raw edges even.
11. Press the seam allowance on the lower edge of the sleeve lining to the inside.
12. Cut two pieces of lace for each sleeve two times the width of the sleeve. Gather one piece of lace to fit the lower edge of the sleeve. Sew to the *wrong side* of the sleeve lining. Gather the second piece of lace to fit about 1" above the edge. Sew this piece in place on the wrong side of the sleeve lining.
13. Sew the lining as you did the jacket, omitting braid. The lace will be on the wrong side of the sleeves when they are set in.

14. Leaving open across the back between the shoulder seams, stitch the lining to the jacket, with the lining on the bottom, next to the machine. Turn and press. Slip stitch back neck opening closed.

NOTE: The trimming added to the jacket may cause the fabric to shrink slightly. By placing the lining material underneath the fabric—rather than on top—you will insure the lining's shrinking-in slightly to match the jacket.

15. Try the jacket on the doll. Following the photograph, mark placement for the ribbon ties: one set should be at the widest part of the bust, one at the waist, and one centered between. Tie in flat knots.

Chemisette

1. Sew darts in chemisette front and in lining front. Press down.

2. Beginning at lower edge, sew the lace ruffling to the chemisette front in rows. You will notice that after you reach the bust dart, the rows will curve; they should.

3. Sew chemisette backs to chemisette front at shoulder. Repeat for lining.

4. Press up seam allowance on lower waist edge of chemisette front and lining front.

5. Right sides together, stitch lining to chemisette, leaving lower front waist edge open to turn.

6. Trim and turn right-side out. Press. Topstitch close to the edge all around.

7. Sew elastic to the front and back at waist edge. Close with snaps.

8. If desired, attach a post earring to the front of the chemisette as in the photograph.

Fashion Engraving from "Godey's"

Hat

The basic shape of the 1850's hat was a rounded crown fit low over the bun in the back, with a slightly rounded brim, framing the face but well back from the forehead.

MATERIALS

Small dish with rounded sides *(I used a dessert dish)*
3″ styrofoam ball
Strips of cardboard
Scrap of fabric *(left-over from stole or dress)*
Maching thread
10″ x 10″ piece of Dip 'N Drape®
Maribou feathers
½ yard ribbon
½ yard lace
White glue
Foil
Oil
Small hatpin

Back of Doll's Hat

Front of Doll's Hat

DIRECTIONS

1. To make the form: cut about 1″ off the styrofoam ball and tape the larger part of the ball off-center to the bottom of the dish. (The dish forms the brim and the ball, the crown.) Tape strips of cardboard between the ball and the dish to smooth out the shape. Cover the form with foil, and oil slightly to ease removal of the finished hat.

2. Wet the fabric and the Dip 'N Drape® and apply to the form. Allow to dry. Keep the crown smooth and distribute the remaining fabric evenly around the rest of the shape. (It does not matter if this is not perfect, as it will be covered with bows, lace and ribbon when it is finished.)

3. After the hat is completely dry, remove it from the form and trim the edges evenly around the brim. Try the hat on the doll. It may be necessary to cut a wedge shape out of the back so that the crown will fit well over the bun.

4. Cut a piece of hat fabric on the bias 1¼″ wide and long enough to fit around brim. Fold in half lengthwise and press. Stitch to the brim through all thicknesses, raw edges together. Glue the folded edge of the bias strip to the inside of the hat.

5. Glue feathers all around the outside of the crown. Glue a lace ruffle inside the brim to cover the folded edges of the bias. Make ribbon ties and bows and glue to the sides. (Hair setting clips make good clamps for holding the trimmings to the hat while the glue is drying.)

6. The hat is not tied on; it is pinned with a hatpin.

The pattern pieces for the dress are on Plates 14, 15, 16, 17 and 18.

Plaid Day Dress

This outfit, like the Blue Brocade Day Dress, is modeled after the engraving on page 16. The pattern pieces are the same, but the braid trim has been omitted and ruching applied after completion. Ruffling has been substituted for the sleeve lace.

MATERIALS

1¼ yards plaid fabric *(at least 40″ wide)*
Matching thread
Hooks and eyes
1 package black seam binding *(for jacket ruching)*
1 yard 3″ ruffling *(for jacket)*
¼ yard white batiste or muslin *(for chemisette)*
2 yards ¼″ white lace ruffling *(for chemisette)*
5 inches ¾″ elastic *(for chemisette)*
Snaps *(for chemisette)*
Post earring for pierced ears *(optional)*

DIRECTIONS

Skirt

1. Cut the skirt 18″ by the width of the fabric.
2. Run a row of gathering stitches along one long side.
3. Measure doll's waist (with corset on) and cut a waistband 1½″ by waist measure plus 1″.
4. Gather the skirt, turning in the seam allowance at the back opening. Pull up gathers to fit the waistband, less 1½″.
5. Allowing a ¼″ overhang at the beginning of the waistband, sew the waistband to the skirt, right sides facing. Press all thicknesses towards the waistband.
6. Turn in and press a ¼″ seam allowance on the long side of the waistband. Fold the waistband in half, lengthwise, right sides together and sew ends. Trim and turn.
7. Slip stitch remaining long end of the waistband to the inside.

8. Sew up back seam and hem skirt. Hem should be just barely above the floor. Close with hook and eye.

Jacket

1. Prepare ruching by running a gathering stitch down the center of the seam binding. Pull up the gathers slightly.
2. Cut one jacket and one lining from the same material.
3. Sew darts in jacket fronts.
4. Sew center back seam. Clip at waist.
5. Join jacket fronts to jacket back at shoulders.
6. Press all seams open.
7. Press seam allowance at lower edge of sleeve to the inside. Attach ruching to the lower edge of the sleeve with edges even.
8. Set in sleeve, sewing with the sleeve on the bottom next to the machine.
9. Sew underarm sleeve seam and the side seam in one continuous seam. Clip at the waist.
10. Press seams open, except for sleeve cap which is not pressed.
11. Press the seam allowance on the lower edge of the sleeve lining to the inside.
12. Cut two pieces of ruffling 9″ long for each sleeve. Gather one piece slightly to fit the lower edge of the sleeve. Sew to the *wrong side* of the sleeve lining. Gather the second piece of ruffling to fit about 1″ above the edge. Sew this piece in place on the *wrong side* of the sleeve lining.
13. Sew the lining as you did the jacket, omitting ruching. The lace will be on the *wrong side* of the sleeves when they are set in.
14. Leaving open across the back between the

shoulder seams, stitch the lining to the jacket, with the lining on the bottom next to the machine. Turn and press. Slip stitch back neck opening closed.

15. Starting at the center back, sew the ruching all around the edge of the jacket. When the end of the ruching is reached, overlap and turn under. Close the jacket at the waist with a hook and eye.

Chemisette

Since the chemisette worn with this dress is the same as that worn with the blue brocade outfit, you can use the same chemisette for both outfits. If you prefer making a separate chemisette for this outfit, follow the instructions on page 16.

Ball Gown

During this era skirts reached extravagant proportions; over 100 yards of material could go into the making of one ball gown which was then worn over a hoop skirt. The doll's ball gown is adapted from another colored fashion engraving from *Godey's* which is reproduced on page 23. Because of the weight of skirts at this time, the dress bodice was usually worn separately. It was laced up the back to keep it very tight and perfectly smooth. If you prefer you can use button loops and tiny buttons. If you wish to use snaps, you must extend the center back of the pattern since the pattern as given will just meet at the center back when completed.

MATERIALS

¼ yard pink cotton brocade *(for bodice)*
½ yard pink chiffon or georgette *(for neck trim)*
½ yard 3″ white lace *(for sleeves)*
1¼ yards pink taffeta *(for skirt and bodice lining)*
8 yards white lace *(for skirt trim)*
6″ thin, embroidered ribbon *(for bodice trim)*
1 yard ¼″ pink ribbon *(to lace bodice)*
Matching thread
Silk flowers and velvet leaves *(for hair ornament)*
Stem wire *(for hair ornament)*
Thin spool wire *(for hair ornament)*

DIRECTIONS

Skirt

1. Cut the following tiers:
   1 tier 15½″ by the width of the fabric
   1 tier 10½″ by the width of the fabric
   1 tier 5½″ by the width of the fabric
2. Fold up a 1″ hem on each tier and press in place.
3. Apply lace to the hemmed edges as shown in the photograph. Use one row of lace on the bottom and top tiers and three rows of lace for the middle tier.
4. With the shortest tier on top, align all of the long, raw edges and run a row of machine basting through all thicknesses of the three tiers.
5. Measure the doll's waist (with corset on) and cut a waistband 1½″ by the waist measure plus 1″.

6. Gather the waist of the skirt, turning in the seam allowance at the back opening. Pull up the gathers to fit the waistband, less 1½″.

7. Allowing a ¼″ overhang at the beginning of the waistband (for seam), sew the waistband to the skirt, right sides facing. Press all thicknesses towards the waistband.

8. Turn in and press a ¼″ seam allowance on the long side of the waistband. Fold the waistband in half lengthwise, right sides together, and sew ends. Trim and turn.

9. Slip stitch the remaining long end of the waistband to the inside.

10. Sew up the back seam and hem the skirt. The hem should be just barely above the floor. Close with hook and eye.

Bodice

1. Sew darts in the bodice front and backs. Trim and clip front dart. Press.
2. Join the backs to the front at the shoulders. Press open.
3. Gather the lace sleeve where indicated on the pattern.
4. Sew the sleeves to the armholes.
5. Sew the sleeves and side seams in one continuous seam. Press open.
6. Sew the lining front and backs the same as the bodice.

The pattern pieces for the ball gown are on Plates 19, 20 and 21.

7. With right sides facing, sew the lining to the bodice around the outside edges, leaving open at the neckline to turn. Trim corners, clip curves and turn.

8. Cut a bias strip 8″ wide by 13″ long from the chiffon or georgette. Fold in half lengthwise and sew across the short ends. Turn. Do not press.

9 Fit a long, raw edge of the chiffon piece to the wrong side of the neckline. Stitch.

10. Turn the chiffon trim to the right side, and gather tightly at center front, shoulders and back. Tack securely to the front at the gathering points. Cover gatherings with your choice of trim. The trim can be embroidered ribbon, as I have used, flowers to match the hair ornament, or even tiny leaves in clusters at the center front and the shoulders.

11. Sew eyelets or tiny buttonholes on both center back pieces.

12. Put the bodice on the doll and lace closed.

Hair Ornament

This flower arrangement was worn towards the back of the head usually fitted around the chignon, and extended slightly past the nape of neck. The doll's curls should be coiled up on the sides and pinned in place to wear with her ball gown and tiara of flowers. Cut a length of stem wire and bend it into a horseshoe shape to the measurement of your doll's head. Using the thin spool wire, attach flowers and leaves to the stem wire.

Fashion Engraving from 'Godey's"

The pattern pieces for the Grecian Cloak are on Plates 10, 11, 12 and 13.

Grecian Cloak

MATERIALS

½ yard velvet, lightweight velveteen or taffeta
½ yard matching lining
Matching thread
2½ yards braid or silk fringe
½ yard ⅜" velvet or satin ribbon *(for neck closure)*

DIRECTIONS

1. Before cutting the pattern for the sleeve, tape the two pattern pieces together.

2. On the back and fronts stay stitch the inward curves as indicated on the pattern pieces. Clip to stitching.

3. Sew the fronts to the back at the shoulder.

4. Run two rows of gathering stitches on the sleeve between the single notch and the "x" at the corner. Pull up to fit between the notch and the "x" on the Grecian-cloak front.

5. Beginning at the lower edge of the back, and matching double notches, stitch the sleeve to Grecian cloak. The sleeve will end at the "x" on mid-front.

6. Sew the lining the same as the Grecian cloak.

7. Clip curved edges where necessary and thoroughly press the Grecian cloak and the lining.

8. Leaving an opening for turning at the lower back, sew the lining to the Grecian cloak around the edge. Clip curves and trim corners. Turn. Press in the seam allowances at the opening in the lower back. Slip stitch closed. Press.

9. Sew braid trim or fringe around the entire outside edge.

10. Cut ribbon in half and sew to front neck edges.

The pattern pieces for the Echarpe Orientale are on Plates 22, 23 and 24.

Echarpe Orientale (Stole)

MATERIALS

½ yard taffeta, tissue-weight faille, lightweight cotton or batiste

Matching thread

1 yard narrow braid or ribbon *(for trim)*

1½ yards ⅜″ ribbon in the same color as the trim *(for ties)*

NOTE: For a dressier stole, you can substitute 2½ yards of 3″ lace for the fabric ruffles, and reduce the fabric requirement to ¼ yard. For the narrower ruffles, trim from the raw edges of the lace to the indicated width. Cut the lengths the same as indicated on pattern.

DIRECTIONS

1. Trace stitching line for the upper ruffle (#3) to right side of fabric.

2. Fold all ruffles in half lengthwise and press. (If ruffles are made of lace, omit this step.)

3. Run a row of gathering stitches along the long, raw edges of the ruffle.

4. Pull up the gathers on the wide ruffle (#4) to fit between the dots on the lower back, matching the raw edges of the stole and the ruffle. Stitch in place.

5. Pull up the gathers on the short ruffles (#1 & #2) to fit between the dots at the front edges and the beginning of the back ruffle just applied. Overlap slightly where ruffle #4 meets. Stitch in place.

6. With the right sides facing, sew the lining to the stole, leaving an opening at the lower back to turn. Clip curves, trim corners, and turn. Press.

7. Pull up the remaining ruffle (#3) to fit along the stitching line marked in Step 1. Stitch in place.

8. Sew the braid from one front edge to the other along the stitching line of the ruffle just sewn to cover the raw edge.

9. Sew ribbon ties to front edges.

Metric Conversion Chart

CONVERTING INCHES TO CENTIMETERS AND YARDS TO METERS

mm — millimeters   cm — centimeters   m — meters

INCHES INTO MILLIMETERS AND CENTIMETERS
(Slightly rounded off for convenience)

inches	mm		cm	inches	cm	inches	cm	inches	cm
⅛	3mm			5	12.5	21	53.5	38	96.5
¼	6mm			5½	14	22	56	39	99
⅜	10mm	or	1cm	6	15	23	58.5	40	101.5
½	13mm	or	1.3cm	7	18	24	61	41	104
⅝	15mm	or	1.5cm	8	20.5	25	63.5	42	106.5
¾	20mm	or	2cm	9	23	26	66	43	109
⅞	22mm	or	2.2cm	10	25.5	27	68.5	44	112
1	25mm	or	2.5cm	11	28	28	71	45	114.5
1¼	32mm	or	3.2cm	12	30.5	29	73.5	46	117
1½	38mm	or	3.8cm	13	33	30	76	47	119.5
1¾	45mm	or	4.5cm	14	35.5	31	79	48	122
2	50mm	or	5cm	15	38	32	81.5	49	124.5
2½	65mm	or	6.5cm	16	40.5	33	84	50	127
3	75mm	or	7.5cm	17	43	34	86.5		
3½	90mm	or	9cm	18	46	35	89		
4	100mm	or	10cm	19	48.5	36	91.5		
4½	115mm	or	11.5cm	20	51	37	94		

YARDS TO METERS
(Slightly rounded off for convenience)

yards	meters	yards	meters	yards	meters	yards	meters	yards	meters
⅛	0.15	2⅛	1.95	4⅛	3.80	6⅛	5.60	8⅛	7.45
¼	0.25	2¼	2.10	4¼	3.90	6¼	5.75	8¼	7.55
⅜	0.35	2⅜	2.20	4⅜	4.00	6⅜	5.85	8⅜	7.70
½	0.50	2½	2.30	4½	4.15	6½	5.95	8½	7.80
⅝	0.60	2⅝	2.40	4⅝	4.25	6⅝	6.10	8⅝	7.90
¾	0.70	2¾	2.55	4¾	4.35	6¾	6.20	8¾	8.00
⅞	0.80	2⅞	2.65	4⅞	4.50	6⅞	6.30	8⅞	8.15
1	0.95	3	2.75	5	4.60	7	6.40	9	8.25
1⅛	1.05	3⅛	2.90	5⅛	4.70	7⅛	6.55	9⅛	8.35
1¼	1.15	3¼	3.00	5¼	4.80	7¼	6.65	9¼	8.50
1⅜	1.30	3⅜	3.10	5⅜	4.95	7⅜	6.75	9⅜	8.60
1½	1.40	3½	3.20	5½	5.05	7½	6.90	9½	8.70
1⅝	1.50	3⅝	3.35	5⅝	5.15	7⅝	7.00	9⅝	8.80
1¾	1.60	3¾	3.45	5¾	5.30	7¾	7.10	9¾	8.95
1⅞	1.75	3⅞	3.55	5⅞	5.40	7⅞	7.20	9⅞	9.05
2	1.85	4	3.70	6	5.50	8	7.35	10	9.15

AVAILABLE FABRIC WIDTHS

25″	65cm	50″	127cm
27″	70cm	54″/56″	140cm
35″/36″	90cm	58″/60″	150cm
39″	100cm	68″/70″	175cm
44″/45″	115cm	72″	180cm
48″	122cm		

AVAILABLE ZIPPER LENGTHS

4″	10cm	10″	25cm	22″	55cm
5″	12cm	12″	30cm	24″	60cm
6″	15cm	14″	35cm	26″	65cm
7″	18cm	16″	40cm	28″	70cm
8″	20cm	18″	45cm	30″	75cm
9″	22cm	20″	50cm		